HEINEMANN
ELEMEN

NORMAN

The Cleverest Person In The World

HEINEMANN

HEINEMANN GUIDED READERS
ELEMENTARY LEVEL

Series Editor: John Milne

The Heinemann Guided Readers provide a choice of enjoyable reading material for learners of English. The series is published at five levels – Starter, Beginner, Elementary, Intermediate and Upper. At **Elementary Level**, the control of content and language has the following main features:

Information Control

Stories have straightforward plots and a restricted number of main characters. Information which is vital to the understanding of the story is clearly presented and repeated when necessary. Difficult allusion and metaphor are avoided and cultural backgrounds are made explicit.

Structure Control

Students will meet those grammatical features which they have already been taught in their elementary course of studies. Other grammatical features occasionally occur with which the students may not be so familiar, but their use is made clear through context and reinforcement. This ensures that the reading as well as being enjoyable provides a continual learning situation for the students. Sentences are kept short – a maximum of two clauses in nearly all cases – and within sentences there is a balanced use of simple adverbial and adjectival phrases. Great care is taken with pronoun reference.

Vocabulary Control

At **Elementary Level** there is a limited use of a carefully controlled vocabulary of approximately 1,100 basic words. At the same time, students are given some opportunity to meet new or unfamiliar words in contexts where their meaning is obvious. The meaning of words introduced in this way is reinforced by repetition. Help is also given to the students in the form of vivid illustrations which are closely related to the text.

Contents

Part One:
MAHMOUD'S LIFE STORY
told by his family and friends

His First Five Years
By Fatiha: his sister   6

His School Years
By Miss Hassan: his teacher   12

His Teenage Years
By Mr Zaki: his official guardian   18

His Early Manhood
By Ali: his best friend   26

His Successful Years
By Aisha: his wife   34

His Year as a Television Star
By Pete Stone: his television
producer   40

Part Two:
MY LIFE STORY told by Mahmoud himself   49

Points for Understanding   59
List of titles at Elementary Level   63

Part One

Mahmoud's Life Story

told by his family and friends

1

His First Five Years

By Fatiha: his sister. My name is Fatiha. I am Mahmoud's eldest sister. My brother was born twenty-five years ago. I can remember that day. I remember it very well.

My mother and father had three daughters. But they always wanted a son.

'Daughters, daughters,' my father often said. 'I only have daughters. They will never help me with my work. They will never earn any money. I don't want any more daughters. I want a son. A son will help me with my work. A son will earn money. I want a son.'

And my mother often said to me, 'Fatiha, your father and I love you very much. We love our three daughters, but we want a son too.'

Then one day my mother said to me, 'I'm going to have another baby, Fatiha. I hope that it will be a baby boy. A boy will help all of us. He will help his father at work. A boy will help all the family.'

I was eleven years old. My sisters were nine and seven. I was very young, but I knew that one day I would marry. My father would need money then. He would need money for my marriage. Later, he would need more money for my sisters.

When a girl marries in my country, her father gives a dowry to his new son-in-law. Some fathers give money. Some give animals. A father also gives things to his son-in-law's family. Rich men give gold and silver.

But my father was not a rich man. We lived in a small village. My father was the village carpenter. He made tables and chairs. My father loved his work, but he was poor. He did not have any animals. And he did not have any gold or silver.

'I have three daughters,' he often said. 'But I have no money, no animals, and no gold. My daughters will have no dowries for their husbands. We are too poor. I need a son. A son will help me. A son will work with me. He will earn money for the dowries. Then my three daughters will get good husbands.'

So my father and mother waited for a son. My sisters and I waited for a brother.

And later that year, Mahmoud was born. Now my parents had a son, and my sisters and I had a brother. We were very happy.

Soon, the whole village knew.

'Come to my house,' said my father. 'Come and look at my son. Come and look at his hands. They're the hands of a carpenter. He will make the best tables and chairs in the country. I know he will.'

'Fatiha,' my mother said to me. 'I am so happy. I have a good husband. I have three beautiful daughters. And now I have a son. One day you will be happy like me. You will have a husband. You will have children too. I hope you have a son, Fatiha.'

I listened to my mother, but I could not stay with her. I was very busy. Everybody in the village came to our house. Then relations came from other villages. There were a lot of aunts and uncles and cousins. They all came to see Mahmoud, my little brother.

I was the eldest daughter. I had a lot of work. I made food and drink for the visitors. I made bread and cakes. I made tea and coffee. There were so many visitors. There was so much work.

'Come and look at my son.'

'Hurry Fatiha, hurry,' my father said. 'You must prepare the food and drink. Our visitors are guests in my home. They must have something to eat and something to drink. Your mother is tired. You must do her work. Hurry! My guests have come to see my son. Now they need food and drink.'

In the days and months that followed, I worked very hard. Often I worked alone. My sisters played with Mahmoud. They did not do much work in the house. And sometimes my mother was very tired. She could not do hard work. She was ill.

And my father did not do any work in the house. He was too busy with his tables and chairs. So I did it. But I did not worry. He was my father, and I was his daughter. He was a man, and I was only a girl.

From the beginning, Mahmoud was not the same as other babies. All babies like to watch and to listen. And all babies like to learn. But Mahmoud was doing these things all the time. He was always learning. He understood what he saw and what he heard. He learnt things very quickly.

Very soon, he was walking. And very soon, he was talking. He was walking and talking on his first birthday! Nobody in our village had seen a baby like him before.

At first, he played with other babies in the village, and he played with my sisters. But soon he stopped playing with other children. He wanted to watch older people. He wanted to listen to them. He spent a lot of time with the men of the village. Mahmoud watched them work. When the men of the village were talking, Mahmoud was there with them. He was always watching, listening, and learning.

I remember one day very well. It was twenty years ago.

Mahmoud was five years old. He was with my father. My father was working. He was making some furniture. He was making some chairs for one of his customers.

I took some tea and cakes for Mahmoud and my father. I heard my father say, 'Look at these chairs, Mahmoud. I have finished them now. They are ready for my customer. The chairs are beautiful. The customer will be very happy with them.'

At that moment, the customer arrived. He looked at the chairs. He liked them. He gave my father some money.

'Thank you,' said my father. 'But this is not enough money, sir. You owe me more money for the chairs.'

'No, I don't,' said the customer. 'I wrote down your prices. I wrote them on this piece of paper. Look. Look at these figures. I don't owe you any more money. I have given you enough money for the chairs. You can read the prices on the paper.'

The customer gave my father the piece of paper. There was writing on the paper, and numbers.

My father looked at the piece of paper. He looked at the writing. He looked at the numbers. But I knew that my father could not read. Mahmoud knew that too. We knew that our father could not understand the words and the figures on the paper. But the customer did not know this. Mahmoud and I did not say anything.

'These figures are wrong,' said my father. He put the piece of paper on a table. 'You owe me more money.'

'No, I don't,' said the customer. 'We talked about the price. I wrote it down. The figures are there. They are on that piece of paper. I don't owe you any more money. I have paid for the chairs.'

My father was angry. He did not know what to say.

But then Mahmoud spoke. He had the piece of paper in his hand.

'The customer is right, Father,' said Mahmoud. 'I have looked at the figures. The customer has paid you enough money. He has paid for the chairs. The figures are right.'

'They are not right,' said my father. 'They are wrong.' He looked at the customer. 'Those figures are wrong. You wrote down the wrong figures. They are not my prices. You owe me more money.'

Now the customer was very angry too.

'I do not owe you any more money,' he said. 'Listen to me. You can keep your chairs, and I can have my money. Or I can have the chairs, and you can have the money. You can choose. What do you want? Do you want the chairs, or the money?'

My father chose the money. He needed the money.

Then my father said, 'Go away Mahmoud. I don't want to talk to you. You did not help me today. I was right, and the customer was wrong. Go away! Go to your mother.'

Mahmoud did not say anything. He walked away. He left my father and me together. My father was very unhappy.

'Mahmoud is my son, Fatiha,' he said. 'But he did not help me today. Before, I was happy, but now I feel sad.'

'Mahmoud is a good boy, Father,' I said. 'I know that he did not help you, but he is a good boy. And he is a clever boy too. He can read. Did you see that? He is only five, and he can read! He has never been to school, and he can read numbers and figures. He is very clever, Father.'

'Yes, Fatiha,' said my father. 'I know that Mahmoud is clever. But I also know that he did not help me today. My son, your brother, is a clever boy who will never help his family.'

Those were my father's words. I have never forgotten them.

2

His School Years

By Miss Hassan: his teacher. My name is Miss Hassan. I was Mahmoud's schoolteacher. Mahmoud was in my school for six years.

My school was a village school. It was very small. There was only one classroom. I was the only teacher.

Twenty years ago, I was a new teacher. I was born in a city. I did not understand village life. I did not understand village people. At first, I did not like the people in the village. They did not like me. I was not married. The people in the village did not like that.

One day, a young woman came to see me. Her name was Fatiha. Her little brother was with her. His name was Mahmoud.

'Excuse me, Miss,' said Fatiha. 'This is my brother, Mahmoud. He wants to come to school. Please may he start school, Miss Hassan?'

'How old is Mahmoud?' I asked.

'He is six,' said Fatiha.

'He is too young for school,' I said. 'He must wait for one year. He may come to school when he is seven years old.'

'But he wants to start now,' said Fatiha.

This was very unusual. Most boys in the village did not want to come to school. They did not like school. But Mahmoud wanted to come when he was only six.

'What do your parents say?' I asked. 'What does your father think? And what does your mother think? Do they want Mahmoud to come to school?'

'Yes, they do,' said Fatiha. 'They want him to start school now.'

I was surprised. Many parents in the village wanted their children at home. They wanted their daughters to help in the house. They wanted their sons to work and to earn money. They did not want their children to go to school.

I went to see Mahmoud's parents. His mother was ill. His father was a tired, unhappy man.

'Mahmoud wants to start school,' I said. 'But he is too young.'

'We know that,' said his father. 'But Mahmoud wants to go to school. He does not want to be a carpenter like me. He wants to learn from books. He does not want to learn from me. I cannot teach my son anything. Perhaps you can teach him something, Miss Hassan.'

'He is a good boy,' said Mahmoud's mother. 'Please let him come to school. That will help us. I am ill. I cannot do much work in the house. Fatiha must do all the work. She must look after Mahmoud. She is busy all the time. When Mahmoud is at school, Fatiha will have more time.'

I thought about Mahmoud's parents. His mother looked very ill. His father looked very unhappy. I thought about Fatiha. She was only seventeen years old, but she looked older. And I thought about Mahmoud. He wanted to come to school. He wanted to learn.

'Mahmoud can start school tomorrow,' I said.

'Thank you,' said Mahmoud's father. 'You are very kind, Miss Hassan.'

'Thank you, Miss Hassan,' said Mahmoud's mother. 'Mahmoud will be a good boy at school.'

'Thank you,' said Fatiha. 'Thank you for your help, Miss Hassan.'

I looked at Mahmoud. He did not say thank you. He did not say anything. He looked at me, but he did not speak.

I have often thought about that day and about Mahmoud's mother, father, and sister. They had told me that Mahmoud was six. They had told me that he wanted to come to school. They had told me that he wanted to learn.

But they had not told me everything. They had not told me that Mahmoud was clever.

———

Mahmoud came to school the next day. But he did not talk to the other children. He did not play with them. He did not sit with them. He wanted to be alone.

I gave him some pictures. 'You can look at these pictures, Mahmoud,' I said.

'I don't want to look at pictures,' he said.

Then I gave him a toy car. 'You can play with this toy car, Mahmoud,' I said.

'I don't want to play with toys,' said Mahmoud.

'What do you want to do?' I asked.

'I want to learn,' Mahmoud replied. 'I want to read and write.'

The other children laughed at Mahmoud. 'You can't read and write, Mahmoud,' they said. 'You are only six. You can look at the pictures. You can play with toys. But you can't read and write.'

'Be quiet, children,' I said. 'I know that Mahmoud is only six. I know that this is his first day at school. But he can watch. And he can listen. We will all do some reading and writing. Mahmoud can sit with us.'

Every day we did some reading and writing. Most of the village children did not want to read and write. Most of them were not very clever. I thought that Mahmoud was like the other children in the village. I thought that he was not very clever.

We had a few reading books at the school. Mahmoud looked at them. He turned over the pages quickly. He did not read slowly, like the other children. I thought that Mahmoud did not understand the words in the books.

I gave Mahmoud some paper and pencils. He wrote things very quickly. I thought that they were pictures. Mahmoud did not want me to see his pictures. He took them home with him.

One day I said, 'Mahmoud, you are not learning anything. You look at books, but you do not read them. You draw pictures, but you do not write words. You told me that you wanted to learn. But you are not learning anything. You must learn to read and write.'

'But I have read those books,' said Mahmoud. 'They are too easy. They are children's books. I want to read difficult books.'

'No, Mahmoud,' I said. 'First, you must read the easy books. You have only looked at the pages. You have not read the words.'

Then Mahmoud said, 'And I can write. But I don't like writing. I like to draw pictures.'

'You can draw your pictures, Mahmoud,' I said. 'But drawing is not writing. You must learn to write. You must watch and listen. Then you will learn.'

From that day, Mahmoud did not like me. He did not watch me or listen to me. When he was at school, he looked at books. I showed him some of my books. Some of them were very difficult! Some of them were in foreign languages. Mahmoud looked at the books. He turned over the pages. Then he gave the books back to me.

On other days, he drew more pictures. I have never seen so many pictures. I knew that Mahmoud did not like me. But I knew that he was happy. All the time he looked at books and he drew pictures. He was a good, quiet boy.

One day, when Mahmoud was twelve, a government inspector came to the school. He talked to me. And he talked to some of the children. He spoke to Mahmoud.

'You are twelve years old, Mahmoud,' said the Inspector. 'Soon, you will be leaving school. You will be a carpenter, like your father.' The Inspector smiled at Mahmoud.

'No,' said Mahmoud. 'I don't want to be a carpenter. I want to be a scientist.'

The Inspector laughed. 'A scientist?' he said. 'But scientists are very clever, Mahmoud. They can read and write. Miss Hassan has told me that you can only read and write a little. How can you be a scientist, Mahmoud? You must stay in the village and be a carpenter. Every village needs a carpenter.'

'Look,' said Mahmoud. 'Look at my pictures.' He gave some of his pictures to the Inspector. The Inspector looked at them.

'Are these yours, Mahmoud?' said the Inspector.

'Yes, they are,' replied Mahmoud. 'Miss Hassan thinks that I am not very clever. She thinks that I cannot read. She thinks that I cannot write. But she is wrong. I can read and write.'

The Inspector looked at me. 'Miss Hassan,' he said. 'You are wrong about this boy. You have not understood him. This boy is very clever. He must leave this school. He must leave you. You have not taught Mahmoud anything, Miss Hassan.'

I looked at Mahmoud. He looked at me. We did not say anything.

3

His Teenage Years

By Mr Zaki: his official guardian. My name is Zaki. I was Mahmoud's official guardian. I looked after him for six years. I first met Mahmoud twelve years ago. He was thirteen.

At that time, I was working in the Ministry of Education. I was a Science Inspector. I travelled round the country. I looked at science classes in schools and I met a lot of people. It was an interesting job and I liked it.

One day, I received a letter from the Minister of Education. The Minister wanted me to go to a village. He wanted me to see a boy called Mahmoud. The letter said that this boy was 'very intelligent and very clever'. The boy was not at school any more. He had left school when he was twelve and now he lived with his family. The letter also said that the boy wanted to be a scientist.

I went to the village. It was very small and poor. I saw the school. There was only one classroom. The village teacher, Miss Hassan, told me something about Mahmoud. But she did not say very much. She said that Mahmoud was clever.

Miss Hassan took me to Mahmoud's family. They were kind, good people. But life was difficult for them.

Mahmoud's father was a carpenter. He worked hard but he was poor. Mahmoud's mother was very ill. I met his three sisters. Fatiha, the eldest, was going to be married soon.

Then I met Mahmoud. He was a tall, quiet boy. I liked him. He told me his name. He said that he wanted to be a scientist.

'But scientists go to school until they are eighteen. Then they go to university, Mahmoud,' I said.

'I know,' said Mahmoud. 'That is what I want to do.'

I laughed. 'I am from the Ministry of Education, Mahmoud,' I told him. 'I have some questions for you. You must answer these questions first. Then perhaps you can go to another school. And one day, you may go to university.

Perhaps you will become a scientist. But first, the questions.'

I gave Mahmoud some questions about arithmetic. Mahmoud had to add, to subtract, to multiply, and to divide. Some of the questions were easy, but some of them were difficult.

Mahmoud's answers were quick, and they were correct. He did not need paper and pencil. I knew then that this village boy was very, very clever.

The next questions were about history and geography. Once again, Mahmoud answered quickly and correctly. None of his answers were wrong. I was amazed. I had never seen any child like him before.

Then I came to the questions about science. Mahmoud's answers were amazing. He knew more than I did. He was the cleverest child I had met.

At the end of the questions, Mahmoud said, 'Can I go to another school? Will I be a scientist, Mr Zaki?'

'Oh yes, Mahmoud,' I said. 'I think that you will be a scientist. But I do not think that you will go to another school.'

'Why not?' asked Mahmoud. 'Why can't I go to another school?'

'You do not need school,' I said. 'You need a university. I think that you will be going to a university, Mahmoud.'

Mahmoud was happy. He looked at his family. But his family said nothing. His father, his mother, and his three sisters did not speak one word.

I went to the Minister of Education. I told him about Mahmoud. I told him that Mahmoud was very clever.

'The boy must go to the university,' I said. 'He will be a great scientist.'

'He is only thirteen years old,' said the Minister. 'When he leaves the village, he will be away from his parents. He will need a guardian. He will need an official guardian.'

'Yes,' I said. 'I will arrange that. I will find an official guardian for Mahmoud.'

'Mr Zaki,' said the Minister. 'I have already chosen an official guardian. It is you. You will look after Mahmoud. You will leave your job today. You are now Mahmoud's official guardian.'

I was surprised. And I was angry. I liked my job. I liked to travel. I liked to visit schools. I did not want to be an official guardian for one boy.

'But Minister,' I said. 'I like my job. Another man can be Mahmoud's official guardian.'

'No, Mr Zaki,' said the Minister. 'You already know the boy. He knows you. He wants to be a scientist. You understand science. You are now his official guardian.'

I was angry, but I could not say anything. I started my new job the next day.

Mahmoud left his village. He became a science student at the university.

I arranged things for Mahmoud. I found a flat for him. I bought his clothes. I bought his food.

I also arranged special lessons for Mahmoud. Mahmoud had teachers from all over the world. One professor said that Mahmoud was the cleverest student he had ever taught. Another professor said that Mahmoud was a genius.

Mahmoud worked hard. He studied all the time. He did

not have any friends. He did not want to go out. He did not like sport. He did not like films. He only wanted to study.

'Why don't you have a holiday?' I said to Mahmoud.

'I don't want to have a holiday,' he replied. 'Perhaps one day I will travel. One day I will see the world. But not now. I want to study.'

It was a strange life for both of us. Mahmoud was a teenager. But he was always alone. He did not like music. He did not want to meet other young people.

I did not like my new job. I never travelled. I never visited schools. I did not meet many people. I only saw Mahmoud. I could not understand his work. We were both scientists. But Mahmoud was a better scientist than I was. When Mahmoud talked to me about his studies, I could not understand him.

Sometimes Mahmoud made me angry. When he was fifteen, his mother died.

'You must go to the village,' I said to Mahmoud. 'Your father needs you. Your sisters want to see you. Your mother has died. Your family is very sad. They need your help.'

'No,' said Mahmoud. 'I will not go to the village. The family does not need me. The village is not my home now. My home is here, at the university. I will not go back to the village.'

Mahmoud did not write to his family. He did not want to see them. When his mother died, Mahmoud did not cry. I did not understand him. Mahmoud was a clever young man, but he was also very strange.

One day, when Mahmoud was eighteen, I had a very important visitor. He was in the army. He was an important military man. I did not know his name, but he knew mine. And he knew about Mahmoud.

'Zaki,' the man said to me. 'I have heard about

Mahmoud. I have heard that he is very clever. I want him to do some work for the army. It is difficult work. It is secret work. We need a scientist. We need him quickly. We want Mahmoud to do this important, secret work.'

'Thank you,' I said to the man. 'I will talk to Mahmoud this evening. I will tell him about this work.'

'Good,' said the man. 'You can tell Mahmoud that we will pay him a lot of money.'

In the evening, I told Mahmoud about the secret military work. 'It will be difficult work, Mahmoud,' I said. 'And everything will be secret. You will not be able to talk about the work to anyone.'

'I can keep secrets, Mr Zaki,' Mahmoud replied. 'I will do the work. I think it will be easy.'

Mahmoud was wrong. The work was difficult. Mahmoud worked every day. He worked in the mornings, in the afternoons, and in the evenings. He became very tired.

And the work was very secret. Mahmoud was allowed to speak to some people from the army, and he was allowed to speak to me. But he was not allowed to speak to any other people. He was not allowed to use the telephone.

One day Mahmoud said to me, 'Mr Zaki, I am tired. I want to finish this secret military work. And I want to leave the university. I have done enough work. Now I have a lot of money. Now I can travel. Now I can see the world. Can I leave the university when I finish this work, Mr Zaki?'

'I will speak to the army and to the Minister of Education,' I said. 'I shall ask them about this.'

I was happy. I wanted Mahmoud to leave the university. I did not want to be his official guardian. I wanted to be a Science Inspector again.

The army and the Minister of Education said that Mahmoud could leave the university. But first he had to finish his military work. Mahmoud worked hard. He finished the work quickly.

He was nineteen. He left the university. He had a lot of money and he bought a flat in the city. He was tired, but he was happy. We said goodbye to each other. I never saw him again.

I went to see the Minister of Education.

'I am not Mahmoud's official guardian now,' I said to the Minister. 'I want to be a Science Inspector again.'

The Minister smiled. 'I'm sorry, Mr Zaki,' he said. 'But you are too old. We need younger men today. I am sorry, but we have no work for you in the Ministry of Education. You must find another job, Mr Zaki.'

I found another job. Now I work in an office. I do not travel round the country. I do not visit schools. I do not meet people. I am not interested in my job. It is boring.

I often think about the six years with Mahmoud, the cleverest student at the university. They were very long years. I want to forget them.

4

His Early Manhood

By Ali: his best friend. My name is Ali. I was Mahmoud's best friend. I was his best friend for two years. I liked him a lot.

I first saw Mahmoud six years ago. One day, I was drinking coffee in a restaurant in the city. I saw a young man in the restaurant. I had never seen him before. He was sitting near me. He was drinking coffee. He was alone. He did not speak to me. I did not speak to him.

The next day, the young man was in the restaurant again. He was alone. I was with some friends. My friends did not know the young man. We did not speak to him.

Sometimes I went to the restaurant alone. Sometimes I went with my friends. Sometimes I went with my sister. The young man was always there. He was always alone.

Then one day when I was alone, the young man spoke to me. 'Hello,' he said.

'Hello,' I said. 'Would you like to sit at my table? We can drink coffee together.'

'Thank you,' said the young man. 'You are very kind.' He came to my table. I ordered some more coffee.

We talked to each other. He told me that his name was Mahmoud. I told him that my name was Ali.

'Where do you come from, Mahmoud?' I asked him.

'I live here, in the city,' he said.

'I live in the city, too,' I said. 'I was born here. I went to school here. But I have never seen you before, Mahmoud.'

Then Mahmoud said, 'I live in the city, but I was born in a village.'

I asked Mahmoud about his family. He did not say very much about them. He told me that his mother was dead. His father was alive and he had three sisters.

'Where do your sisters live?' I asked.

'I don't know,' said Mahmoud.

'You don't know?' I said.

This surprised me. In our country, we know everything

about our families. We always talk about them. But Mahmoud did not know much about his family. And he did not want to talk about them.

'No, Ali,' said Mahmoud. 'I don't know where my sisters live now. I never see my family, and they never see me. I do not want to talk about them.'

I did not ask any more questions about Mahmoud's family.

Then Mahmoud asked me, 'What is your job, Ali? Where do you work?'

'I am a student,' I replied. 'I am a science student at the university.'

Mahmoud said nothing. I thought that he was not interested in science. I said, 'And you, Mahmoud? What do you do?'

'I was a student too,' he said. 'I was at the university. But I have finished my studies now.'

This was another surprise for me.

'But you look very young, Mahmoud,' I said. 'How old are you?'

'I am nineteen,' he said.

'And you have finished at the university?' I said. 'I am nineteen years old too. But I am in my second year. And I have never seen you at the university.'

Then Mahmoud looked at me. 'I was a special student,' he said.

Then I remembered. I remembered about a special student at the university. I had heard about Mahmoud. I had heard about a very clever student. I had heard that he had done some secret work. The work was for the army. The army had paid the special student a lot of money.

'I have heard about you, Mahmoud,' I said. 'A lot of

people talk about you, but they have never met you.'

Mahmoud smiled. 'Yes, Ali,' he said. 'Everybody has heard about me, but nobody knows me. Nobody knows that I am lonely, Ali.'

'Lonely?' I said. 'But why are you lonely, Mahmoud?'

'I have no friends, Ali,' he replied. 'I was studying for many years. I was working for the army. It was secret work. I do not know anyone, Ali. I have no friends.'

'Mahmoud,' I said. 'I shall be your friend. You can come home with me. You can meet my family. My parents and my sister will be happy to meet you.'

Mahmoud was very happy. 'Thank you, Ali,' he said. 'You are very kind. But I must ask you one thing, Ali.'

'Anything, Mahmoud,' I said. 'You are my friend. Ask me anything.'

'Please do not tell your family about me,' replied Mahmoud. 'Do not tell them who I am. Do not tell them that I was the cleverest student at the university.'

I laughed. 'I will not tell them,' I said. 'But they will soon find out, Mahmoud. You are very clever. You know many things. People will soon learn that you are clever, Mahmoud.'

Mahmoud laughed. 'Perhaps,' he said. 'But we will not tell them. It will be our secret, Ali. It will be a secret between friends.'

Mahmoud paid for the coffee. I saw that he had a lot of money. Then I took him to my home.

Mahmoud came to my house. My family liked him. My father often talked to Mahmoud. One day, my father said to me, 'Ali, I like your new friend Mahmoud. He is very clever. He knows a lot about science.'

'Yes,' said my mother. 'I have talked to Mahmoud about music. He knows a lot about it.'

My sister Aisha was sixteen. She liked Mahmoud too. Sometimes Mahmoud helped Aisha with her school work.

'I am learning many things from Mahmoud,' she said. 'He is very clever. He helps me to understand my school work. I like your friend, Ali.'

Mahmoud helped me too. He helped me with my studies. I finished my second year at the university. I started my third year. Mahmoud helped me to study. He helped me to learn. He helped me to understand science. He was my best friend.

One day Mahmoud said, 'Ali, when you leave the university, what will you do? What job will you take?'

'I don't know,' I said. 'Perhaps I will be a teacher.'

'That is a good idea,' said Mahmoud. 'But I have a better idea.'

'What is your idea, Mahmoud?' I asked.

'We can travel,' said Mahmoud. 'We can go round the world, Ali.'

'But I haven't got any money,' I said.

'I have lots of money,' said Mahmoud. 'I will pay for you.'

'Oh, thank you, Mahmoud,' I said. 'You are very kind. But where will we go? Which countries will we visit? What will we do?'

'Let me show you,' said Mahmoud. 'Look at these letters, Ali. They are from all over the world.'

Mahmoud showed me the letters. There were some letters from France. There were some letters from England. There were some from South America.

'What are these letters, Mahmoud?' I asked. 'Who are they from?'

'They are from radio and television companies,' said Mahmoud. 'I wrote to radio and television stations all over the world. And they wrote back to me. These letters are their replies.'

'But why did you write to all these radio and television companies, Mahmoud?' I asked. 'Do you want to be on radio and television?'

I laughed.

'Don't laugh, Ali,' said Mahmoud. 'Yes, I do want to be on radio and television. I want to be on radio and television all over the world!'

'But what will you do?' I asked.

'I will take part in competitions,' replied Mahmoud. 'All of these radio and television companies have competitions, Ali. I will take part in them.'

'What sort of competitions are they?' I asked.

'Competitions for clever people,' replied Mahmoud. 'There are competitions for clever people in France, in England, and in South America. There are competitions in countries all over the world. And I can win these competitions. I can become the cleverest person in the world.'

I thought about Mahmoud's idea. I knew that he was clever. I knew that he could answer difficult questions.

'It's a good idea, Mahmoud,' I said. 'I will come with you. I will help with the arrangements. I will arrange the journeys and hotels. You can win the competitions.' We both laughed.

'Yes,' said Mahmoud. 'We shall go round the world together. And I will become the cleverest person in the world.'

We planned our journey. We made all the arrangements. Mahmoud wrote to a lot of radio and television companies.

I wrote to a lot of hotels.

Sometimes my sister helped us. 'I want to come with you,' she said.

'You are too young,' I replied.

Soon I finished my studies at the university. Mahmoud and I were ready for our journey. I was very happy. I wanted to see foreign countries. I wanted to travel. I wanted to travel with my best friend, Mahmoud.

I arranged to meet Mahmoud at the airport. I went to the airport. But I did not find Mahmoud. He was not at the airport.

He had gone. He left me a note.

The note said:

Dear Ali,
I have started my journey. I have taken your sister, Aisha. We shall be married soon. Thank you for your help.
Your friend,
Mahmoud.

My best friend had gone without me! He had taken my sister. He was going to marry her.

My mother and father were very angry. We never talked about Mahmoud again.

5

His Successful Years

By Aisha: his wife. My name is Aisha. I am Mahmoud's wife.

I first met Mahmoud when I was sixteen. He was my brother's best friend. He often came to our house.

Mahmoud helped me with my school work. I thought that he was very kind. I fell in love with Mahmoud. I wanted to see him all the time. I wanted to be with him all the time.

I did not tell my family that I was in love with Mahmoud. My parents never knew that I was in love with him. My brother never knew that I was in love with his best friend.

One day, I heard about Mahmoud's plans. He told me that he wanted to travel. He told me that he wanted to be the cleverest person in the world.

I did not want Mahmoud to leave me. I told him that I was in love with him. He told me that he was in love with me. We were both very happy. But we did not tell anyone that we were in love.

Mahmoud and Ali made their plans. Ali wanted to travel round the world with Mahmoud. He did not know that Mahmoud would take me.

I did not want to leave my family. I did not want to leave my country.

'Mahmoud,' I said. 'We must tell my parents that we are in love. We must tell them that we want to be married.'

'No, Aisha,' said Mahmoud. 'We must not tell them. They will not let us marry. They will not allow me to take you round the world. They will want you to stay at home. They will want me to stay at home with you. But I want to travel, Aisha.'

Mahmoud wanted me to travel round the world. I wanted to tell my family that we were in love.

But I did not tell them. I left my country, and I left my family. I was eighteen. Mahmoud was twenty-one. I loved him very much.

Mahmoud and I went to France. That was two years ago. We were married in Paris. I liked Paris. I liked the shops. I liked the people. But I often thought about my own country. I often thought about my parents.

One day Mahmoud said, 'Tonight, Aisha, I will be on the radio. It is my first competition. I hope that I will win. The winner will get a lot of money, Aisha.'

Mahmoud did win the competition. It was his first success. The questions were about science. Mahmoud thought that the questions were easy.

Soon Mahmoud was on the television too. He took part in two more competitions. He won them both. He won a lot of money. Mahmoud was becoming very successful.

'These competitions are easy for me,' said Mahmoud. 'I know all the answers. I will win a lot of money. I am the cleverest person in France, Aisha!'

Mahmoud was very happy. Everybody wanted to see him. Everybody wanted to meet him. Everybody wanted to talk to the cleverest person in France.

'Soon we will go to England, Aisha,' said Mahmoud. 'They have a lot of competitions there.'

We went to London. I liked London very much. I visited theatres and cinemas. But I was often alone. Mahmoud was very busy. He was on the radio and the television. He took part in many competitions and won them all. He was very successful. He was happy.

'Aisha,' said Mahmoud one day, 'I am the cleverest person in England. I have won many competitions and I have won a lot of money.'

'Yes, Mahmoud,' I said. 'You are a success. But I do not see you very much now. You are always working hard.'

'I must work hard,' said Mahmoud. 'I want to travel to more countries. I want to travel round the world. I am the cleverest person in France and in England. Now I want to be the cleverest person in the world, Aisha. Soon, we will go to South America. I can win a lot of money there.'

I did not want to go to South America. I wanted to go home and see my family. I wanted to see my parents and my brother, Ali.

'No, Aisha,' said Mahmoud. 'You cannot go home. Your family has never written to you. They do not want to see you again. You have left your country. You have left your family. You are my wife now. You must stay with me, Aisha. You must come with me to South America.'

'But I want to go home,' I said to Mahmoud.

'Aisha, you cannot go home,' he said. 'You have no money, and you are my wife. I have our money, and I am your husband. I am taking you to South America, Aisha.'

We went to South America. We visited many countries.

Mahmoud was successful everywhere. He was very popular. Everybody wanted to meet him. People called him 'the cleverest person in South America'.

But I was unhappy. I did not see my husband very often. I wanted to go back to my country and see my family again.

I said to Mahmoud, 'You are successful and rich. Now we can go home.'

'No, Aisha,' said Mahmoud. 'I do not want to go home. I do not want to see my family. They do not know me now. They do not know that I am successful. They are in their village, and I am here. I will not go back.'

'But you can see my family, Mahmoud,' I said.

'Don't be silly, Aisha,' said Mahmoud. 'Your parents will be angry with us. Your brother will be angry too. No, I do not want to see your family or my family, Aisha. I like to travel. I like to win competitions. And I want to be the cleverest person in the world.'

One day, a man came to see Mahmoud. The man was an American. He said his name was Don Hardman.

'I have heard about all your successes,' said the American. 'Everybody says that you are a very clever young man.'

'Thank you, Mr Hardman,' said Mahmoud. 'This is Aisha, my wife.'

'Your wife?' said Mr Hardman. 'I did not know that you were married.'

Mr Hardman did not speak to me. He wanted to speak to Mahmoud.

'Well, Mahmoud,' said Mr Hardman. 'I am from New York. I work for a big television company. I have an idea for a new programme. It is a competition. The name of the competition will be *The Cleverest Person In The World*. Will you take part in this competition, Mahmoud?'

'*The Cleverest Person In The World?*' asked Mahmoud. 'Who will take part in the competition, Mr Hardman?'

'There will be people from many countries,' said Mr Hardman. 'My company is sending me all over the world. I am looking for very clever people. The winner of our competition will be the cleverest person in the world.'

'What sort of competition will it be?' asked Mahmoud.

'There will be questions on all kinds of subjects, Mahmoud. There will be questions about science, about music, about literature, and questions about a lot of other subjects too.'

Mahmoud looked at me. Then he looked at Mr Hardman. 'Yes,' said Mahmoud. 'Yes, Mr Hardman. I will go to America. I will go to New York. I will take part in your competition. I want to win. I want to be the cleverest person in the world.'

'Good,' said Mr Hardman. 'It will be a great competition, Mahmoud. It will be the best competition in the world. I will see you in New York. Goodbye, Mahmoud.'

'Goodbye Mr Hardman,' said Mahmoud.

Now my husband was very happy. 'This will be my biggest success, Aisha,' he said.

'But I do not want to go to America, Mahmoud,' I said. 'The competition will be very difficult. You may not win. Then you will be very unhappy.'

'I will win,' said Mahmoud. 'I know that I will win.'

'But I do not want to go to America,' I said again. 'I want to go home.'

'No, Aisha,' said Mahmoud. He was very angry. 'We are not going home. We are going to America. We are going to New York.'

'Then you must choose, Mahmoud.'

'Choose?' said Mahmoud. 'What do you mean, Aisha?'

'You must choose our country, or America. You must choose your wife, or Don Hardman. You must choose love, or success. Choose, Mahmoud.'

'But I don't want to choose,' said Mahmoud.

'But you must choose,' I said.

Mahmoud chose America, Don Hardman, and success. He did not choose our country, his wife, or love.

My husband gave me some money, and said goodbye. That was two years ago.

6

His Year as a Television Star

By Pete Stone: his television producer. My name is Pete Stone. I was Mahmoud's television producer.

I was the producer of a television show. The show was called *The Cleverest Person In The World*. It was made in New York.

My boss was Don Hardman. He travelled all over the world. He went to Africa, Asia, Europe and Australia. He travelled all over America. He was looking for the cleverest people in the world. He wanted these people to be in his show.

One day, nearly two years ago, Mr Hardman told me about Mahmoud.

'He is a very clever man,' said Mr Hardman. 'I met him in South America. He is now here in New York. He wants to be the cleverest person in the world. Go and see him Pete. Go and talk to him.'

I went to see Mahmoud. I liked him. Mr Hardman was right. Mahmoud was very clever. I wanted Mahmoud to be in our competition. And Mahmoud was young. He was good-looking. I knew that the audiences would like him.

I spoke to Mahmoud about the competition. 'The show will start later this year,' I said. 'I am making the arrangements now.'

'Good,' said Mahmoud. 'I need time. I want to read. I want to learn more before the show. I want to win your competition, Mr Stone. I want to be the cleverest person in the world.'

'Then we must make the arrangements,' I said. 'I want to talk to you about three things. I want to talk to you about your name, your clothes, and your money.'

'Why do you want to talk to me about my name?' said Mahmoud. 'What is wrong with my name?'

'There is nothing wrong with your name, Mahmoud,' I said. 'It is a very good name. But for Americans, it is a difficult name. Americans cannot say your name. We need another name. We need an easier name. I think that we will call you *Shafeek*.'

'Shafeek?' said Mahmoud. 'Do you want to call me Shafeek?'

'Yes,' I said. 'On television, we will call you Shafeek.'

'And that will be my television name?' asked Mahmoud.

'Yes,' I said. 'Now I want to talk to you about your clothes.'

'My clothes?' said Mahmoud. 'What is wrong with my clothes? Why do you want to talk to me about my clothes?'

'You will be a television star,' I said. 'I want your clothes to be interesting. People will want to see something different.'

'Something different?' asked Mahmoud. 'What do you mean?'

'Your television name will be Shafeek,' I said. 'Your television clothes will be different too. We will dress you like a prince.'

'But I am *not* a prince,' said Mahmoud. 'I do not want to wear a prince's clothes.'

'Why not?' I asked. 'We can call you Shafeek the Prince. The audiences will love that. They will remember that name. Everybody will want to see you. You will be very popular.'

'How many people will watch the show?' asked Mahmoud.

'Millions,' I said. 'Everybody in America will want to see *The Cleverest Person In The World*. It will be a very successful show, Mahmoud.'

Then Mahmoud said, 'All right, I will wear a prince's clothes. I will be on the show. I will be on the show as Shafeek the Prince.'

'Good,' I said. 'Now the third thing. Money. We must arrange your money, Mahmoud.'

'Yes,' said Mahmoud. 'How much will you pay me?'

'Every competitor will get the same,' I told him. 'But the

best competitors will get more. And the winner of the competition will become very rich.'

Then Mahmoud said, 'I don't want any money.'

I was amazed. 'You don't want any money! But everybody wants money. Why don't you want any money, Mahmoud?'

'I have enough money,' he replied. 'A long time ago, my government gave me a lot of money. Then I won some money in France, England, and South America. I don't need any more money. I don't want any more money. Mr Hardman can keep his money. I only want to win. I only want to win your competition, Mr Stone.'

I was pleased. I had a clever competitor. I had a good-looking competitor. I had asked him to change his name, and he did change it. I had asked him to change his clothes, and he did change them. And Mahmoud did not want my money!

I made more arrangements for the show. I saw all the other competitors. Soon, everything was ready.

The Cleverest Person In The World started last year. The

show was on American television every Friday night.

At first, the show was not very popular. One day, my boss said to me, 'Pete, I'm worried. Not many people are watching the show. The questions are too easy. The competitors are not very interesting. We're losing money.'

'Don't worry, Mr Hardman,' I said. 'Next Friday, Mahmoud is on the show. I think that people will like him. We call him Shafeek the Prince.'

Mahmoud was a great success on his first show. He answered all the questions quickly. All his answers were right. He was the best competitor that week.

After the show, we had a lot of telephone calls.

'Shafeek the Prince is good,' one person said. 'I hope that we shall see him again.'

'Shafeek was the best person on the show,' said another caller. 'I want to meet him.'

'I call him Shafeek the Super Prince!' said another caller. 'I hope that he wins the final competition. I hope that he will become the cleverest person in the world.'

A few weeks later, Mahmoud was on the show again. The same thing happened. He was the best competitor. He was the cleverest competitor. He was the most interesting competitor.

The show was a great success. 'Now I'm very happy, Pete,' said my boss, Don Hardman. 'Mahmoud, or Shafeek, has made the show a great success. Everybody in America watches the show. They like the show. They like Shafeek. We are making a lot of money now.'

Mahmoud was a star. Shafeek was the most popular person on television. Everybody wanted to meet him and talk to him. And everybody wanted him to win the final show.

One day Mahmoud said to me, 'I like my new name now. I like the clothes. I like being Shafeek. Everybody knows me, and everybody likes me. Thanks for everything, Pete.'

'And I thank you too, Mahmoud,' I said. 'You have made my show successful. Without you, *The Cleverest Person In The World* would not be a popular programme. The final show is next week. Everybody in America will be watching it. They will be watching you and the other competitors. The winner next week will become the cleverest person in the world!'

'Yes,' said Mahmoud. 'I hope that the winner will be me. I want to become the cleverest person in the world, Pete.'

I laughed. 'I know, Mahmoud,' I said. 'But we must wait and see. The questions will be very hard. All the competitors are reading more books this week.'

'I know,' said Mahmoud. 'I will read some more books too. Goodbye, Pete. I will see you next Friday.'

'Goodbye, Mahmoud,' I said.

Then I prepared for the last show. It was the final. Everything was ready.

The night before the show, I went home very late. I was tired. I went to bed. But a few minutes later, I got up. There were two men at the door. One was Don Hardman. The other man was Mahmoud.

'Hello, Mr Hardman,' I said. 'Hello Mahmoud. What do you want? It's late.'

Mahmoud did not say anything. But Mr Hardman said, 'Pete, let's go inside. Mahmoud wants to ask you something. He wants to ask you something about the final show.'

I took them inside and we sat down.

'What do you want to know, Mahmoud?' I asked.

Mahmoud looked at me. 'I want to know the questions for the final show.'

'The questions?' I said. 'You can't see the questions, Mahmoud. They are secret. The other competitors have not seen the questions. And you cannot see them. That would be wrong.'

'But I want to win,' said Mahmoud. 'I want to be the cleverest person in the world.'

'I know, Mahmoud,' I said. 'But you cannot see the questions.'

'Listen, Pete,' said Mahmoud. 'I have done everything for you. I changed my name for you. I changed my clothes for you. I did not ask for any money. Now you do something for me. Give me the questions before the show.'

'No, Mahmoud,' I said. 'I will not give you the questions.'

'Pete,' said Mahmoud. 'Give me the questions, or I will leave the show. Without me, there is no show. The show will not be a success without me, Pete. You will lose money. You will lose your job.'

I looked at Don Hardman. 'Is that true, Mr Hardman?' I asked.

At first, Mr Hardman did not speak. But then he said, 'Yes, Pete, that is true. We need Mahmoud. The show needs Shafeek. Give him the questions, Pete.'

'But Mahmoud is very clever,' I said. 'He does not need the questions. He is cleverer than the other competitors. He will win the final. Mahmoud does not need the questions now.'

'I do need the questions!' shouted Mahmoud. 'The other competitors are very good.' Perhaps I will not win the final. Give me the questions.'

'Give him the questions,' said Mr Hardman. 'Give him the questions, Pete, or leave your job.'

'Listen, Pete, I have done everything for you.'

I could not leave my job. I needed the money. I could not leave the show. It was my most successful show.

I gave Mahmoud the questions. They were difficult questions. But Mahmoud was very clever. He knew all the answers.

The next night, Mahmoud was on the final show. He won. Shafeek became the cleverest person in the world.

Part Two

My Life Story

told by Mahmoud himself

'Good evening, ladies and gentlemen. Welcome to our late night TV show: MY LIFE STORY.

Each week, we ask a famous person to tell us the story of his or her life. Then we ask six members of the audience to meet the famous person.

This week, our guest is very famous. You have seen him many times on TV. He is the cleverest person in the world. His name is Shafeek.

Tonight, Shafeek, the cleverest person in the world, will tell us his life story.'

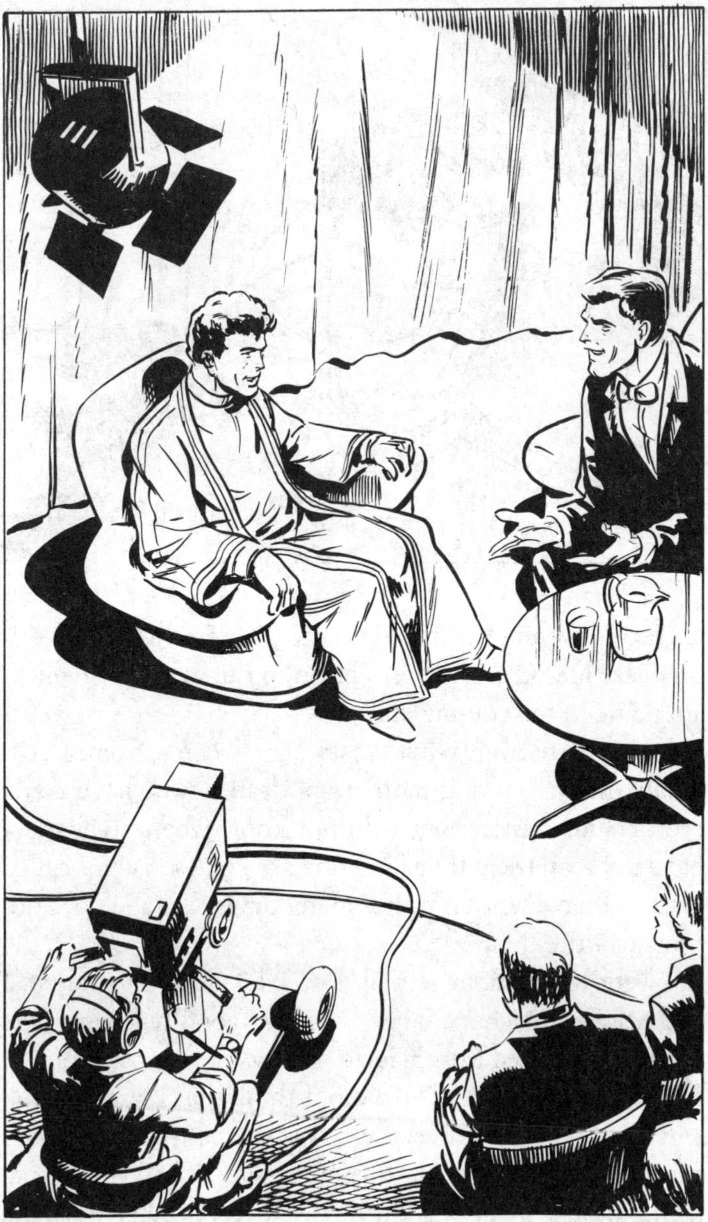

Good evening, ladies and gentlemen. My name is Shafeek. I am the cleverest person in the world. Tonight, I am going to tell you my life story.

I was born twenty-five years ago. I come from a rich family. My father and mother are dead now. I have many brothers and sisters, but I do not know where they are. I have not seen them for a long time. My eldest sister is called Fatiha. I have written to her many times, but she does not want to write to me.

I went to a famous school. I was the cleverest student. I had a lot of teachers. They were not good teachers. One teacher was called Miss Hassan. She was a very bad teacher. She did not help me. She did not think that I was clever.

Then I went to university. I was the best student. I was the cleverest student at the university. I had an official guardian. His name was Mr Zaki. He never helped me. He always wanted me to work hard. He wanted me to work for the government. I think that Mr Zaki is dead now.

I left the university. I did not know what to do. I had a friend. His name was Ali. He wanted to travel round the world. I wanted to travel too. We made plans. We wanted to travel round the world together. But then Ali got a job. He did not tell me. I went round the world alone.

I loved Ali's sister. Her name was Aisha. She was very beautiful. I asked her to marry me. But she said no. She did not love me.

I went to France, to England, and to South America. I won many competitions. I became the cleverest person in those countries. Then I came to America. I became a television star. My producer was Pete Stone. He was the producer of the show, *The Cleverest Person In The World*. I was the star of the show. Pete liked me. He wanted me to win the show. Once, he wanted to show me the questions. It was before the final show. But I said no. I did not want to see the questions. I said that I would win the show.

And I did win the show. And now I am the cleverest person in the world.

'Thank you, Shafeek. That was very interesting. We now know a lot more about the cleverest person in the world.

Shafeek has told us the story of his life. Six members of the audience can now come up and meet Shafeek.

Now we have six members of the audience with us. They are going to meet our guest.'

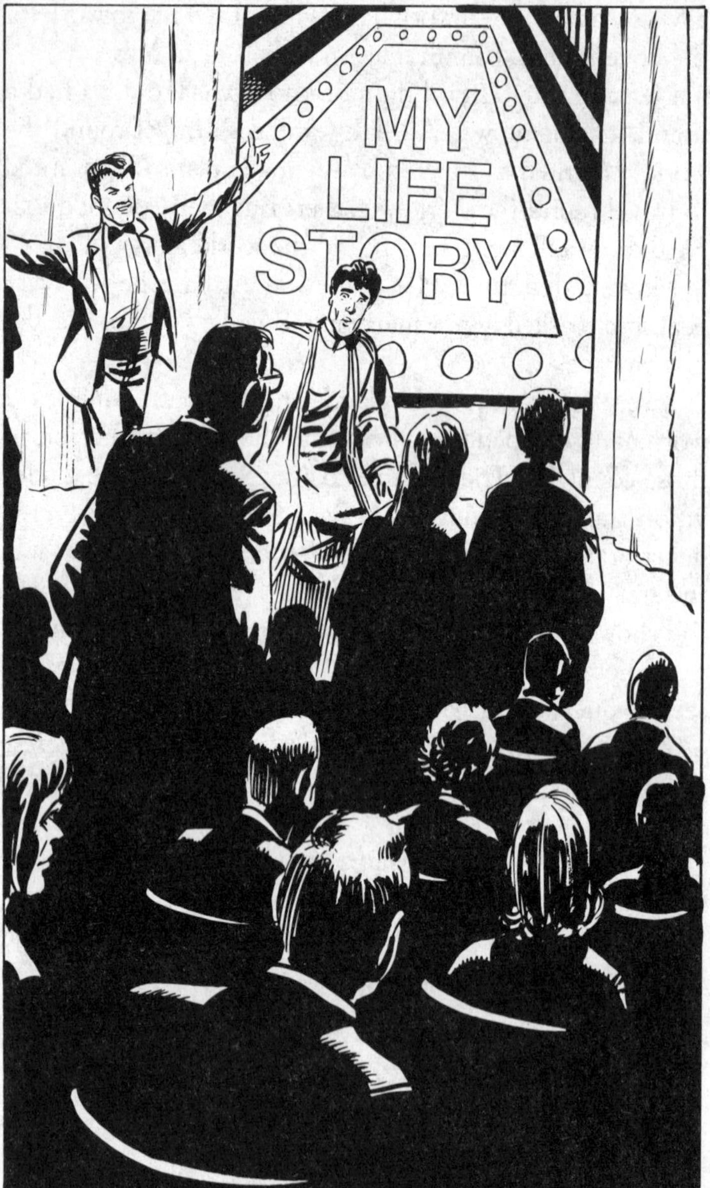
MY
LIFE
STORY

My name is Fatiha. I am the eldest sister of the cleverest person in the world. Mahmoud, I gave you my childhood. I want my childhood, Mahmoud.

My name is Miss Hassan. I was the teacher of the cleverest person in the world. Mahmoud, I gave you my books. I taught you many things. I want thanks, Mahmoud.

My name is Zaki. I was the official guardian of the cleverest person in the world. Mahmoud, I gave you my life. I gave you all my time. I want a job, Mahmoud.

My name is Ali. I was the friend of the cleverest person in the world. Mahmoud, I gave you my friendship. I want a friend, Mahmoud.

My name is Aisha. I am the wife of the cleverest person in the world. Mahmoud, I gave you my love. I want love, Mahmoud.

My name is Pete Stone. I was the television producer of *The Cleverest Person In The World*. Mahmoud, I made you a star. I want the truth, Mahmoud.

Go away, all of you. I cannot give you those things. I will not give you those things.
Go away, all of you. I will not give you anything.
I cannot give you your childhood, Fatiha.
I will not give you thanks, Miss Hassan.

I cannot give you a job, Mr Zaki.
I cannot give you a friend, Ali.
I will not give you love, Aisha.
I will not give you the truth, Pete.
Go away, all of you.

Points for Understanding

PART ONE

1

1 Fatiha's father had three daughters. Why did he want a son?
2 What did Fatiha have to do when Mahmoud was born?
3 From the beginning, Mahmoud was not the same as other babies. How was he different?
4 Who did Mahmoud spend a lot of time with?
5 How did Fatiha learn that Mahmoud was able to read?
6 Was Mahmoud's father pleased with his son's cleverness?

2

1 Mahmoud's family wanted the boy to go to school. Why did this surprise Miss Hassan?
2 What did Mahmoud's family not tell Miss Hassan?
3 Why did the other children laugh at Mahmoud when he first came to school?
4 Miss Hassan thought that Mahmoud was not able to read or to write. Why did she think so?
5 Miss Hassan gave Mahmoud some books.
   (a) What did Mahmoud say about them?
   (b) What was Miss Hassan's reply?
6 The inspector came and looked at Mahmoud's drawings. What had Miss Hassan not understood about Mahmoud?

3

1 Mr Zaki told Mahmoud: 'I do not think that you will go to another school.' Why not?
2 The Minister of Education made Mr Zaki Mahmoud's Official Guardian. Why was Mr Zaki angry?
3 Mr Zaki said: 'Sometimes Mahmoud made me angry.' How did Mahmoud make Mr Zaki angry?
4 'You can tell Mahmoud that we will pay him a lot of money.'
    (a) Who was going to pay the money?
    (b) What kind of work was Mahmoud going to do?
5 What happened to Mr Zaki when Mahmoud left him?

4

1 Where did Ali first meet Mahmoud?
2 What did Mahmoud tell Ali about his family?
3 What had Ali heard about Mahmoud at University?
4 Ali took Mahmoud to meet his family. What did these members of Ali's family say about Mahmoud: Ali's father? Ali's mother? Ali's sister, Aisha?
5 'But I have a better idea,' Mahmoud told Ali.
    (a) What were Ali's plans for the future?
    (b) What was Mahmoud's 'better idea'?
6 'Look at these letters, Ali,' said Mahmoud.
    (a) Who were the letters from?
    (b) What were the letters about?
7 Ali did not find Mahmoud at the airport. What had happened?

5

1 Aisha said to Mahmoud: 'We must tell my parents that we are in love.' What was Mahmoud's reply?
2 Mahmoud and Aisha went to France.
   (a) What did Aisha do there?
   (b) Was she happy?
   (c) What did Mahmoud do there?
   (d) Was he happy?
3 Mahmoud and Aisha went to London.
   (a) What did Aisha do there?
   (b) Was she happy?
   (c) What did Mahmoud do there?
   (d) Was he happy?
4 Did Aisha want to go to South America?
5 Aisha wanted to go home and see her family.
   (a) Why did Mahmoud not want to see his family?
   (b) Why did Mahmoud not want to see Aisha's family?
6 Who came to see Mahmoud in South America? What did he want?
7 Aisha told Mahmoud: 'Then you must choose.'
   (a) What did Aisha mean?
   (b) What choice did Mahmoud make?
   (c) What happened to Aisha?

6

1 What was the name of Pete Stone's television show?
2 Pete Stone told Mahmoud: 'I want to talk to you about three things.' What were the three things?
3 Was Pete Stone's show a success at first?
4 Late one night, Mr Hardman came with Mahmoud to speak to Pete Stone.
   (a) What did Mahmoud want?
   (b) Why did Pete Stone give Mahmoud what he wanted?

PART TWO

1 In his life story, Mahmoud told many lies. What lies did he tell about:
   (a) his family?
   (b) his sister, Fatiha?
   (c) his school?
   (d) his school teacher?
   (e) his university career?
   (f) his guardian?
   (g) his friend, Ali?
   (h) Ali's sister, Aisha?
   (i) Pete Stone, the television producer?
2 Six people came up to speak to Mahmoud at his television show. They each asked for something.
   (a) Who were the six people?
   (b) What did each one want?

A SELECTION OF GUIDED READERS AVAILABLE AT
ELEMENTARY LEVEL

Road to Nowhere *by John Milne*
The Black Cat *by John Milne*
Don't Tell Me What To Do *by Michael Hardcastle*
The Runaways *by Victor Canning*
The Red Pony *by John Steinbeck*
The Goalkeeper's Revenge and Other Stories *by Bill Naughton*
The Stranger *by Norman Whitney*
The Promise *by R.L. Scott-Buccleuch*
The Man With No Name *by Evelyn Davies and Peter Town*
The Cleverest Person in the World *by Norman Whitney*
Claws *by John Landon*
Z for Zachariah *by Robert C. O'Brien*
Tales of Horror *by Bram Stoker*
Frankenstein *by Mary Shelley*
Silver Blaze and Other Stories *by Sir Arthur Conan Doyle*
Tales of Ten Worlds *by Arthur C. Clarke*
The Boy Who Was Afraid *by Armstrong Sperry*
Room 13 and Other Ghost Stories *by M.R. James*
The Narrow Path *by Francis Selormey*
The Woman in Black *by Susan Hill*

For further information on the full selection of
Readers at all five levels in the series, please refer
to the Heinemann Guided Readers catalogue.

Heinemann International
A division of Heinemann Publishers (Oxford) Ltd
Halley Court, Jordan Hill, Oxford OX2 8EJ

OXFORD LONDON EDINBURGH
MADRID ATHENS BOLOGNA PARIS
MELBOURNE SYDNEY AUCKLAND SINGAPORE TOKYO
IBADAN NAIROBI HARARE GABORONE
PORTSMOUTH (NH)

ISBN 0 435 27198 9

© Norman Whitney 1979, 1992
First published 1979
Reprinted four times
This edition published 1992

All rights reserved; no part of this publication may be
reproduced, stored in a retrieval system, or transmitted, in any
form or by any means, electronic, mechanical, photocopying,
recording or otherwise, without the prior written permission of
the Publishers.

Illustrated by John Richardson
Typography by Adrian Hodgkins
Cover by Matthew Richardson and Threefold Design
Typeset in 11.5/14.5 pt Goudy
by Joshua Associates Ltd, Oxford
Printed and bound in Malta